SIXTEEN

POETRY COMPOSITION 01

ELLE BLUE

Special Thanks To:

All the people who stoked the fire and pushed
me to get this done—you know who you are.

My cover designer! Not only did you nail my vision,
but seeing your beautiful illustration was the first time
this whole "I'm publishing a book!" process felt real.

My big sister, for always supporting
me, no matter what.

My very first patrons on Patreon!

and lastly,

All the people who have followed Known
as Blue and all of its iterations.
(You know y'all are hype!)

Dedicated To:

All the odd little girls full of heart and hope and
passion, who feel lonely, lost and misunderstood.
I see you, I hear you, I was you, I am you.

And for 14 year old me; the brave, broken and
wondrous little girl who started this whole thing—
you will always live inside me.
I hope I made you proud.

Introduction

Sixteen was born sixteen years ago, and I wish I could say that that synchronicity was intentional. But that would be too perfect, and as we all know, or at the very least come to learn; art and life never go as planned.

I first started writing this book in the winter of 2003, though I didn't yet know it would become a book, one that I would end up filling with over 150 poems. I was 14 years old and living a sheltered life of some highs and many lows—I had divorced parents, a hoarded home, a narcissistic mother, and assorted compliments from boys (and far too many men) that I didn't want or know what to do with. But I also had a few close friends I adored, tons of creative outlets, a super cool older sister, and the suburbs of New York as my playground. And above all this, I had a beat in my head. And I felt compelled to get it out.

I was attending the Freshman Center, a cramped former elementary school housing only ninth graders, in what felt like a last, rushed hurrah before being separated again in High School the next year. They'd corralled all the 14 and 15-year-olds from the four middle schools in town, which meant that 3/4 of my schoolmates were kids I'd never seen before. I was also on crutches for the third time, which meant hobbling to classes after the bell rung, the whole room turning to look at me as I entered a few minutes late every period. I lived close to the school, so I was a walker, but because of my precarious predicament, I was assigned a short bus that would pick me up every morning and drop me off every afternoon. If I ever woke up late and missed my ride (or did *any other thing* on *any given day*, really) the wrath I faced from my mother was often physically and emotionally devastating.

I quickly determined that school was going to be a bit alienating, but unfortunately home was no better. My mother seemed to up the ante in her crazy that particular year: re-introducing an abusive ex-boyfriend into our lives, dragging me to worship at her church of the moment, and neglecting not only me and my siblings but also our dog who was chained to a tree in our backyard—a fact that broke my heart every time I went back there to feed him.

I felt anxious, helpless and overwhelmed by all of my life's changes: newly painful periods, new braces, successive surgeries on my feet, perplexing feelings on an almost daily basis. I struggled to keep my grades up while I juggled my chaotic home life and my frazzled mind. It was as insane as it sounds. The direction in which my world was changing seemed above my threshold of knowledge. I had very little resources and didn't feel like I had anyone to turn to. But worst of all, I knew there was next to nothing I could do about it.

I physically escaped my house as often as I could, going to friends houses, movies, restaurants, parks, and the beach. But when I wasn't allowed to leave, I turned my innermost feelings *further* inward, making it a remarkably creative year for me: I aced all the projects in my studio art and animation classes, attaining perfect scores and winning awards left and right. I journaled almost daily, madly; many of my entries reading like wild screeds of my ever-changing moods and interests, whole days jotted down in unusual detail that no one else could decipher. I began penning short stories about imaginary kids who were just like me. And I started writing poetry during boring classes (5th period was especially productive), during all the times I had to sit out of phys ed, and in my neatly organized bedroom that overlooked my quiet street.

Back then, these poems were born out of flashes of inspiration that hit me in the spare moments my mind wasn't cluttered with worries, chores or homework. I was often struck with a lightning bolt of a line that I just *had* to get down before it escaped me forever. (I'm positive that I lost a few excellent lines because I couldn't get to a pen fast enough!) I never thought about why I was getting these ideas, or why I was writing them down. I just did. And it was so exhilarating that it was easy to keep going. When I was a teenager, I would continue to do almost *anything* if it was fun!

Now, I know that it was a channel for my loneliness, my despairs, my vulnerabilities. The page was the ever listening ear that I didn't have in real life. A place to express my fantasies, my desires, the things that I felt and the many many things I hadn't yet, in a space of non-judgment.

I wrote about my crushes, pain and my real life (*Superstore, *The First Time, *Friday-Night-Poet, *Not Tonight), and things that I enjoyed (*Amusement, *A Summertime Memento, *Heat). I incorporated various elements that inspired me (I borrow the Shel Silverstein line "All the magic I have ever known, I've had to make myself" in one of the poems, I reference the former Virgin record store in New York City's Union Square neighborhood in *The First Time and *El Baile del Amor Latino was inspired by my Latin culture). Some topics came from the farthest depths of my mind (*Particles I, II, III; *Stagefright, The 'Colors' Poems), and others came straight from the Lifetime Channel (*Concept of a Broken Marriage, *Peace, *Burning Pages).

Art, expression, but especially poetry saved me. I leaned on it like a crutch, writing feverishly from ninth grade well into High School. I never wrote poetry again after that.

I named the book "Sixteen" for the median age in which the book was written. But for years, this collection of poems was a simple black and white composition notebook with the word 'Poetry' scrawled on the front. It sat quietly with my dozen or so journals, and came with me when I moved to New York City at 19, as well as the billion times I moved after that. This poetry book was one of my most cherished possessions, I had barely let anyone read it and I certainly never intended to publish it.

It was only when I sat down to read it again, over a decade later, that I realized the gem I had. My soul stirred as I read the words I had penned so long ago, and I knew if these words resonated so strongly with me, they could impact other readers similarly.

I'm ready to share this part of me now, and I think the worried, beautiful, spirited teenage girl I was back then would be okay with that. But most importantly, I think she would be overjoyed at what she has unknowingly done, she achieved an accomplishment that now benefits both of us.

So here it is. My teenage poetry book in its (mostly*) original form. I hope it provides as much joy for you as it did for me.

---

* A handful of poems were left out to spare my scholarly embarrassment, and a handful were edited for clarity/typos.

*Friday-Night-Poet

It's gotten so late tonight
it's my usual routine
and I've chosen to write
cause my drawing is starting to suck
and that's when I know it's time

I've done a lot this week
surprised myself this week
But I'm bare tonight
with nothing but the pages of poetry
no ones but mine
my life in its entirety
only written in rhyme

There's a mirror across the room
and I get a reflection of me
a talented young poet
and a skinny little thing

It's Friday night
and no one has called to hang out
but I ain't feelin' lonely
I'll just chill in my room
and maybe write some more poetry...

2/21/03

*Individuality

There are so many
of those types
because that's what
we are told to be like
You are the different chick
the weird sort of type
sometimes you just don't connect
it's hard for you to follow the hype
you want the attention it's clear
though you say you feel alone
not sure what resides up "there"
I think you're a gem, not a stone
but it doesn't matter what I think
'cuz that's the way you are, and will always be
others' opinions can cause you to sink
so I suggest keep doing your own thing
or whatever makes you happy

*Untitled

Feeling lonely once again
It is so familiar to me
like a best friend
What does it mean?
Love
Where did it go?
Love
What happens now?
Where do I turn
Where do I look
to find the one...

Safe from the hurt
Save for some tears
I wonder how he's feeling now
every he I've found...

Love
Where did it go?
What happens now?
Where do I turn
to find the one...
Where do I look
to find the sun

*One Drop at a Time

They're like raging rivers
pouring out of my eyes
it just keeps going
(One drop at a time)
One drop at a time

Seeing your face
and seeing hers right next to
I collapse inside
(One drop at a time)
One drop at a time

Flashing back to the day
you held me after
explaining your love for me
had ran away

I just let it flow
(One drop at a time)
Just let it go
(One drop at a time)

(ONE DROP AT A TIME)

*Flattery

I know I'm getting
noticed, as I walk
down this busy city
street. It makes me
laugh. I feel four
eyes on my body, as
I enter the quaint little
coffee shop, it makes
me blush. I hear you
say that I'm beautiful,
as I take the seat across
from you. It makes
me cry.

1/23/03

*Teen Angst

I am a teen/it makes me sad to say/this
period in my life I have begun to hate/I feel
so confused/so abused/so unsure/I can't take
anymore/I'm about to blow/with what/I don't
know/I just wanna grow up/in both ways/not in
one.

1/23/03

*Milk-Chocolate Poet

You're in my English class and when you read
I get shivers down my spine. You've got milk
chocolate skin and you're a gentleman. You have
dark coal eyes like diamonds and you're sweet
like sugar, playful like me and a fun spirit that
dances when I'm around. You're a damn good
poet, real good for a guy and a pearly smile. You
got the perfect guys teen name and you wear
Hawaiian shirts a lot. You're not like anyone I
know and you're good. And when you're good,
you are *good*, I know. I could gaze at you for
hours, and you could tell me all your stories. I
would like that; yeah.

1/23/03

*Player

How lovely is/your tender smile/it makes my butterflies/go completely wild/just hearing your voice/gets me excited/a feeling I have/I just can't fight it/It's unstoppable/the way it feels inside/thinking with my heart/not with my mind/I cannot speak/I am so blind/what a player/I cannot speak/he's got me blinded/what a player.

1/23/03

*Yesterday's Gone

Don't you wish that
you could say to me
how you were sorry
how you didn't mean it
Those harsh cold words can never be taken back.
Yesterday's Gone
Can't turn it back now, too late now, too late
Don't you wish that you hadn't said goodbye??
'Cause yesterday's gone and so am I.

1/23/03

*The People's Song

Feeling so much hate inside/ready to burst/
anger oozing out of my eyes/remembering
the hurt/What affects me most is pain/my
angst/will not be slain/these piles of emotions
amassed/will now be smashed/Why does
everyone go after me/What is it that I did/They
see a girl like me/and want her to pay for her
sins/feeling so much hate inside/ready to burst/
anger oozing out of my eyes/remembering the
hurt/memories don't fade/my life will always be
a dark shade.

1/23/03

*Untitled

Every time I see you
I'm left mesmerized
and this feeling inside
if you must deride
you're making me high
every time you talk to me
I'm left hypnotized
I don't know why
I don't think you know
your capability and how
you work those eyes
you do so much to me
but still I'm so confused
'cause your signals aren't
clear and I don't know how you feel...
Could you explain??

1/23/03

*Untitled

Do you remember me??
Think back a few years,
our summers together
up at our tree house
and those nights we
rambled on
and on and on
But you don't
and it hurt
more than you know
to think I'd found an old friend
and found nothing
instead.

1/23/03

*Gonna Be Okay

You try that on/it doesn't fit/you wear that
shirt/that looks like shit/the day has passed/
you got nothing done/he hasn't called/since
day one/it's all gonna be okay/okay-baby/ok
yeah/You spilled your milk/tried not to cry/
You tripped and fell/those heels were too high/
the day has passed/You got nothing done/your
stockings are the wrong color/and they've got
a huge run/it's all gonna be okay/okay-baby/
gonna be okay/ok yeah.

1/23/03

*Untitled

When I see you
I end up
missing what we had
questioning my decisions
and your mysterious motives
Oh I wish it was easy
to take you back.
But my pride
makes it too difficult.
More than I can bear.

1/23/03

*Untitled

I used to get letters from her all the time
and then she stopped
She used to call me all the time
but then she stopped
I can't forget what we used to be
How could she throw it all away?
I used to get hellos and I cannot
understand why she's changed
How could I forget
what we used to be??

1/23/03

*Untitled

I wish I could know
what you're thinking
on the rare occasion
that you're just like me
(crazy).

1/23/03

*Insecure

I'm sitting at a desk
with obscenities etched
all over it
my lips are chapped
and three girls ask me
what I am
I look down at my
ratty sneakers and
hope the cute guy
a few seats away
hasn't noticed them yet,
or noticed me at all
cause after all
I look like
trash.

1/23/03

*Dreaming of You (Happy)

It's 2 AM
and I'm sprawled out on my bed
thinking of you
and I'm wondering if you are doing the same
and I wish I was with you right now
and I just wish that for one night
we could lie in silence
and just be happy with the fact
that we are beside each other
with a love so deep and true and strong
I wish I could hold you in my arms forever
and tell you how much I love you
and tell you that we have to be together
and I wish
that for one simple night
I could lie with you
and you would put your big strong hands
around me
as if silently telling me
that you are my protector
and that you'll always be there
and that you are so proud to have me
as your girl.

1/25/03

*Untitled

I spent all day thinking
about you
and me
and all the possibilities
it's so overwhelming
but how could there be
a you and a me
if you're so in awe of her.

*Untitled

Your harsh cold words
whip me around
like a strong wind
on a cold day
And so I let them take me
and I take in the chill of their meaning
and I want to laugh at you
and tell you that you're not hurting me
But the tears in my eyes
might give me away.

You strike me hard
like a lightning bolt
on a stormy night
And so I let you take me
and I take in the pain of your hit
and I want to scream at you
and ask you why you're doing this
But the fear on my face
might give me away.

You grab me
with the power of a wave
in an empty ocean
And so I let you take me
and I take in the bruise of your grip
and I want to cry and tell you to let me go
But the weakness in my body
might give me away.

You hold me close
and say you love me
like you're supposed to
And so I let you take me
and I take in the warmth of your touch
and I want to cry and tell you it can't be this way
But the smile on my face might not ever
give me away.

1/25/03

*Drunken Love (Getting Over You)

Getting over you has been so hard...
Where do I start??

Oh I must've tried a thousand times
My oh my how time has flied
Asking myself how and possibly why
Has this guy got me hypnotized.

Constantly on my mind
Telling me strange secrets and lies
But never spending more than a moment's time.

You gave me love
Showed me innocence
And what I could never be
Never your true love
And you held me
And expressed your necessary sympathies.

Pride cannot be broken down
It wouldn't let me touch you
At last I had banished the sound
Of your voice, your call, your cries too.

The bright hue of our love
Has faded to a solemn black
I fell in love
And scarred myself at that.

Your twisted desire
Hidden by your eloquent charm
Had me hooked like a drug
Even though you did me so wrong.

You had a clever way of making it all shine
As I fell rock hard for your every line
Your persistence clouded my motivation
To break free from this false elation.
I honestly never thought this could be
Such a perfect thing as you and me
I remember that night when you bet
That I sparkled even in my rest.

The way you still manage to make me smile
Even though the smiling hurts
And then you walk away in heart and mind
With your love for me still undefined.

I admire how you can kiss me
And it still feels good
You must be possessed
Cause whatever you're giving me
Has got me left—obsessed

Your touch I can still feel
It lingers around on my body
Those lonely days still make me cry
And my heart is still fawning.

And I have no idea why
I'm letting you touch me this way
Love me this way
How do I let you act this way??

As if it never happened...
As if it were never said...
And today
you apologized
and kissed me passionately
and I realized
that I have never been farther away
from true love

I left this drunken love sober
I am finally over...

*Untitled

I say it's not that serious
although I wish it was
if only you could see
the white picket fences
crystal clear in my dreams.

*An Ode to Inner Beauty

You thought you were beautiful
as they had told you so
but how strange that is
because for this same reason,
you believed you were horrible.
The spirit in which
you need to revive,
lies deep inside.
Those compliments do not help,
if you do not believe it
within yourself.
Beauty on the outside
is not a permanent thing,
inside of you,
the thought must remain true,
let your beauty ring.
When you express your feelings
and emotions and thoughts,
that's when you will truly shine.
A genuine person
realizes this,
and admires your strength
so fine.
Pay close attention
to the person that's inside,

if it's ignored,
rest assured,
that your inner beauty dies.
Walk in confidence
and hold on tight,
finding what's inside
can be a crazy,
bumpy ride.
Be careful not to fret
and let all know
that in your happiness
you're set.
So do not let them
fool you with those words
so harsh and quick,
because all wise persons know
that outer beauty does not stick.
Next time you are told
that you are simply divine,
inside yourself you'll know
that it is both
in heart
and mind.

2/3/03

*Untitled

Will there ever come a point in life
where there's nothing left to talk about?
Where the world has lost its wonder?
Where everything has been said and done?
Will there ever come a time in life
where you've lost your magical abilities?
Where you've written every poem?
When every thing you say is cliché?
Will there ever come a period in life
where you would understand it all?
Where smiles are no longer free?
When the stars stop shining?
Will there ever come a day in life
where nothing is unique?
Where nothing is genuine?
Where nothing is full of passion?
Only if you let it.

2/3/03

*Blonde Hair Beautiful

There was this girl I once knew
She had this twinkle in her eye
Blonde hair beautiful
She was so different
So open minded
She was the one
So inspirational
So special
Blonde hair beautiful
She was my reason for living
I loved her with all my heart
I never loved anyone like her
She was blonde-haired
and beautiful.

2/15/03

*Break Up

Every time you stare I'm there and I
can't believe that nothing's going right
I place my hand on top of your shoulder
I recognize that this could be so over
I contemplate the words that I have sent you
the kisses, hearts, deserved a pretty faced fool
My own heart guides me to the wrong place
look in the mirror can't recognize my own face
I wonder whether it was plenty worthwhile
I cry inside and tell myself to be mild
I stone the witches that live inside me
I curse the world for knowing how to shake me
The room is dead I'm not sure if I'm breathing
I laugh, damn this life is sure deceiving
explain the reason why you left me
can you tell me why you're hesitating
see now my love is disintegrating
things are easy when the sun is shining
explore the meaning of your words boy
Don't lie you used me as a love toy
I can't help but think I'm on the brink of it all
it's hard enough to just pick up and swallow
There's another girl in your midst now
make sure you're nice and keep your vows
you're dreaming like you'll never wake up
I hope one day you'll regret the break up.

*Untitled

Wonder what the world has for me
whether you have company
crying inside
but the tears don't seem to fall
wanting to be loved
I know it ain't that far
I know one day I'll rest
and my life will be so blessed
I'll be so certain of everything
that I'll be humming melodies

2/15/03

*The Sinister Solo

I am playing the song of my life
long, sad, solemn notes
with my head down
watching this old violin
and my scarred hands
play out my sadness
Rough, strong and hard strokes
play out my anger
my pent up rage
all let loose through my music
through this piece
Played out with such intelligent vigor
and the crowd goes wild
at the end of the last note
I get a standing ovation
for playing only what my life
has thrown at me just moments before.
I breathe in deep
and observe the smiling crowd
realizing that what I just did
was all because of
this crazy, bad, and horribly
unforgiving day.

2/15/03

*El Baile del Amor Latino

Hot...
Smoky...
Humid afternoons...
Sweet Spanish Summer.
Sweet Summer days
on the rooftops of the city's apartments
which overlook our tiny neighborhood.
The hot, sinister sun beating down on our bodies
as if keeping with the rhythm
of the old salsa discs that play
in the background.
The sizzle of the barbecue
and the refreshing sprays of the water hose
accompany the sounds of giggling children
and *viejos* playing dominoes.
Everybody is dancing real nice and slow
as if making way for the soft breeze
that carries the fresh scent of Latin love.
We get into the beat
and move to the sounds of a lonely guitar
along with the 'swish swish' of my red dress.
I smile at the thought of finding true love
in the Spanish delight of your embrace
and of my culture.

2/21/03

*Untitled

You smell like my favorite beach
I like to learn what your kisses teach
You know that you're my one and only
I like how you speak, so soft and slowly
You have real nice eyes
Like the moonlight in disguise
You don't dance, you sashay
Take my hand, I'll show you the way
You think one day our hearts will blend
in time I wanna be your best friend
You love me at no expense
to you my mind makes perfect sense
And isn't that why I love you?
Isn't that why I said "I do"?
Your hand holding mine is a privilege
With our lives entwined
that's how we live.

2/21/03

*Untitled

Baby I can agree
you're an idol to me
can you say I'm obsessed
or that I'm simply a mess
I say it's definitely
that you are after me
but I can't act
like I'm not falling like that
and I can't say
that I don't see
that look you give me
after we've been kissing.

*Untitled

We're in this weird situation
that doesn't allow us to be
in that type of connection
if you know what I mean

There's that one girl you've got in a spell
and your deep infatuation with somebody else
and I'm sorry, but I can't act as if
I'm definitely not attracted

But imagine if some way
it were possible
that we were rid
of those obstacles

How much we could hang out
How much we could laugh and "play"
How much I would be kissing you
how long you would allow me to stay

But right now we can't make progress
unless you wanted to
We would have to keep that quiet
I'm sure you would like that, wouldn't you?

So right now we can choose
whether we decide to be
friends or enemies
but being "just friends"
would surely be tempting.

2/21/03

*Untitled

make me breathe
make it rise
make me cry
make a sound
tell me you're having fun
with your mouth
slide it in
nice and slow
here we go
come with me
to ecstasy
feels too good
make sure it should
move around
make a sound
of utter joy
blow me away
say it's okay
I'm glad you're mine
I think I can fly
because of you
who loves me so
enough to share
this intimate moment.

*Untitled

I rip your picture off my wall
I don't even care at all
I don't know what you've done
I dunno where you been
all I know is that this is the end
and I won't even shed a tear
cause man, you're not worth it
and I don't even care.

*Not Easy

>making peace with you
>is not as easy as I thought
>making love to you
>is not as easy as I thought
>making it all for you
>is not as easy as I thought.

*Untitled

I'm scared
and so unprepared
as this feeling took me over
I wasn't ready
I was too young
for a relationship this serious
for a relationship this strong
I was a naive little girl
thrown out into the world
I had never felt a love like this
something that I didn't know what to do with
Don't get me wrong
Yeah it was fun
but I was dumb
I'm sorry love
How would I know if it was definite
could this be for real?
At this age
change is common
and I can't afford
to be broken down
broken up with
or just plain
broken.

*Untitled

This color red
excites my
little soul may
you be with me
forever and
never let me go.

*Imagining

I felt a breeze the other day
and it was chilling, but so refreshing
and I let it take me
and I imagined that breeze
had lifted me up and away
and had set all my troubles aflame
but when I turned around
I was still next to you
waiting to be dumped.

*VIRUS

Close the door
and lay here
and I'll make you
wonder
what I'm up to
and you'll
talk to me
and say anything
that comes to mind
'cause that's all you can
think to do
when I'm loving you
and you'll get up
and stand tall
and try to act like
I'm not getting to you
at all

and you won't even know
what hit you
'cause in a few
you'll be backing down
and I'm telling you
there's no remedy
get out now
while you can
before you get sick
if you can
it all depends
on how fast you are
if I even let you leave
how fast can you run
before you catch
the virus?

*Untitled

Go ahead and light your candles
they're not that bright anyways
ashes overflow the mantle
and you're asking me to stay
the kitchen is practically deserted
the place is colder than my heart right now
you can't believe I'm so assertive
and I can't help but give you a scowl
Go ahead and turn your music on
but don't make up anything else
all the magic I have ever known
I have had to make myself
I'm feeling really sick right now
in this "romantic" atmosphere
I can't even think about how
I'm getting out of here
You dropped me off at home "Yeah thanks!"
but don't expect me to call
this relationship definitely sank
before it could begin at all.

2/23/03

*Pretty Young Jeans

The streets are cold
we're on the sidewalk
the moon is nowhere to be seen
I'm holding your hand and tonight
I'm in my pretty young jeans
the ones you like
I burn inside when you slip
your hands in my back pockets
and hold my body close to yours.
I rest my head on your chest
and you pick my chin up with your hand
and kiss me.
And thinking back now,
I wonder if you would've kissed me
if I wasn't in my
pretty young jeans.

*Untitled

Can you tell me how
you're working this, baby?
This sick, sweet enrapture?
And can you clarify
how you stole my freedom
with only that look in your eye?

*Silence

Everyday it stays the same
a silence of night still detained
I beg from you the love that's lost
I wish we could just sit and talk

Instead you stay enveloped in silence

Just another mindless feat
a world of silence you see
I believe that our love is lost
I don't want to pay the cost

Instead you stay drowned in silence

Maybe my life has gone
You've been so very silent for so long
I thought our love would last
I think that the "us" has passed

Instead you stay silent.

*Rain

Hard splash
cold drops
of rainwater
hit the ground
compelled to gather
together
and fall
into small
circular
puddles
making a flood...
it's raining outside today
and it's the first time
I don't mind.

*Gone

Different places
Different faces
life's not fair
when you're not here
then last night
I saw your face
heard your voice
had my last taste
my tongue is raw
from trying to speak
the words you couldn't hear.

*Untitled

Too busy making sure
that you were happy
put all of me aside for you
I would've died for you
for 16 long years
I kept that up
now that you're gone, what do I do?
'cause I never knew how to live
unless it was for you.

*Untitled

Tired of looking over
other people's shoulders
butting into
what I don't belong
I would like to say
one day
that
I have my own extraordinary love.

*Morning

Can't wait
to see your face
in the soft glow of the morning
as you lie there breathing in deep
you amaze me with your peaceful sleep
The white sheets cover our bodies
letting me explore what's underneath
You know you look so beautiful this early
you are so sexy when you speak slowly
Are you making me want you
without saying a word
How are you so magical
without even trying to?
It must be morning.

*Summer Things

It's cute what June brings about
cute little summer things
that have waited all year to sprout
and cement their roots into ground
until winter comes and pulls them out.

*Untitled

Snow flurries in your coffee cup
can't say that crying is a must
but that's all I'm compelled to do
after being with you
Rainwater has been leaking through the pipes
I hold back tears with all my might
upon my pillowcase was where I wept
within my dreams your presence had crept
Wind makes the trees billow on this clear day
I don't remember saying that you couldn't stay
I wonder how I've gone all these days without you
stuck within this spellbound rue.

*Untitled

I lied
when I said I was crying
over some guy
when you know who
it was about
'cause it was you
Yeah I put you aside
but you did the same to me
so why should I apologize?

*Red is the Green is the Blue
is the Black is the Gray

Red
is the passion that lingers
is the blood on my fingers
the color of the flame
the way you say my name.

Green
like the color in your eyes
that favorite shirt you wear all the time
the color of the grass we lie on
as you tell me talking to him is wrong.

Blue
Like all the bruises left on my skin
like the heavenly skies you said love lived in
a tear upon your light cheek
Like the ocean breeze I wish would take me

Black
the darkness we whispered in our first night
the smoke after the candlelight
like the twisted turmoil of our sea
was the death of you and me

Gray
is a scary, but blissful stormy day
in a strand welcomes old age
is the body below the tombstone
are the shadows only seen when the light's shone

*Particles

Melted pieces of blue sky
confined to one small area
expressions and kisses goodbye
tell me where is my savior?
These words I scribble down
in vain, that pretty silly frown
across your face
you know it can't stay too long
and they dare and ask
if it's worth the task
I'm frantic
I panic
in my hotel room
with my amethyst luggage going zoom
along the ride behind me.

*Your Dark Chocolate Eyes

Standing there stripped of my skin
cuz your dark chocolate eyes
leave me helpless
and wanting to cry
This impending guilt over me
has taken away my dignity
and your dark chocolate eyes
give no sympathy
meshing all your threads
entwined with mine
like a quilt full of colors
sewn by your dark chocolate eyes

*Untitled

I can't believe I'm missing you so much
even though you're not gone
and all these feelings and such
are just too strong
and it's hard to get over
I kept fighting pure spunk
hard to get sober
when you're always feeling drunk

*Untitled

I hear you're a legend
Yeah, it's all around town
you're a lover with lessons
and I want them right now
Let's waste no time waiting
wondering what to do
Let's waste no time saying
"What about me and you?"
So why don't we get together
and we'll have our fun
'cause it's important to remember
tomorrow is promised to no one.

*Untitled

Your dark skin
your sneaky smile
I love your wit
it makes me wild
So much about you
makes this easy
I hear you can dance
I'd like to see thee
The way you act
and play around
makes me want to know
will you be mine now?

*Particles II

Sitting on this old, firm bed
depression looming in and out of my head
but mama's picture is on the nightstand
saying if I need it, she'll give me her hand
On the walk to the audition place
that blue guitar over my shoulder
the expression on the judge's face
made me steam all over
not that I like it
not that I fight it
but there was nothing I could do
'cept go home and decide I'm through
It's been a cold cold winter
but nothin' like today
I've been told I have the eyes
of a darling princess
yeah, well I'll be it if you ask.

*Untitled

nothing is sweeter than
writing my own story
creating my own legend
keeping touch with my future
and letting the world know
I'm their company.

*Rich in Love

We are just the beginnings of
a naive little story
a palace full of glory
that's you and me
the King and Queen

We live our lives without surrender
and gaze at our abundant splendor
and spend all the time in the world
with each other
because you're my royalty
and I treasure you
like no one else.

*Doomsday

The weekend went too quick
I'm feeling a little sick
and it's Monday
my jacket's too warm
and there's gonna be a storm
later today
Could I have picked
a better way to say this?
Could I have picked
a better day to say this?

*Particles III

Serenity doth bringeth the night
and a handful of moths aflight
cool calm and collected is my light
Heading back down the trail to home
where my dreams lay
shielded, unopened, unknown
This guy at the bus stop had a look
that was my token
to decide and stay and make my way
yes I will make it work
I will never let go of my dream
unless a lot of stuff comes up
but for now I'm here on the floor
looking at my life
the strife
the plight
the fight
in nothing but particles.

*Stage Fright

I'm sitting here
at this café
I'm in the slums
but I must play
Got my guitar
strumming along
get into the groove
the beat's so strong
I'm singing loud
from deep within
the place smells of smoke
and it's itching my skin
the music takes me over
my heart beats fast
clock strikes ten
will this feeling last?
I'm feeling kind of wild

I like the sound we make
the crowd is real excited
how much can they take?
there are some faces in the crowd
who are really enjoying it
everybody's up and going
and I can barely sit
it's all going good
till I freak out
"What the hell went wrong?"
my bandmates shout
I thought I saw him in that dark corner
and suddenly my face got warmer
I tried to keep playing with all of my might
but I failed myself and this is
just another case of stage fright...

*Carry On

Pick up the pieces
move yourself onward
dust yourself off and
take the weight off your shoulders
smile big and bright and
walk upright
hold your head up high
and realize
it'll be alright.

*Sad, Sweet, Sour

You've been sad, sweet and sour
and I won't ever be the same
every sentence, every last word drips
with the soft whisper of your name
Dreaming about you, me and what I've missed
the way we could've touched,
the way we could've kissed
you were my heart, you were my thoughts,
I was you
and all I'm left with
are these sad, sweet and sour memories...

*White is the Yellow is the Violet
is the Orange is the Pink

White
Like the pure thoughts in your mind
the wispy clouds that float in the sky
like the scent of vanilla orchids
are the doves that fly in the wind

Yellow
like the golden strands in your hair
like the lemons life sometimes throws here
you always reflect me at my best
is the sun that sets in the west

Violet
like the fragrant lilacs that in winter go unseen
cause you are my King and I am your Queen
like the grapes that grow upon the vine
the darkness that midnight brings by

Orange
Like the blaze in the fire, bright with color
is citrus, tart like no other
like the spice in the journey we call life
is the way you seem to glow all night

Pink
are my cheeks cause you make me blush
is little girls frilly dresses and such
is giggling with your friends until you hurt
was the lipstick on your button down shirt.

*Untitled

Passion fire heat desire
caused my body to be weak
aching for his presence
reaching for his hand
his body-rocking love
that in the end
left me craving more
he saw our love
and he wanted it just as bad
my body was in submission
and more in lust than ever before
So he was perfect
could you be better?

*Deep in Like

My eyes divert
to a soft spoken
abstract guy in the corner
I draw closer
the place gets warmer.
My Spanish lips smile
for his luscious eyes
and to my surprise
I fell deep into like.
I can't be blamed
'cause his words are
spoken with eloquence
complete with a smile
underneath.
'Cause I fantasize
about his lips
now preoccupied
with telling the stories
of his life.
'Cause I can't get him
off my mind and that
should be reason enough
to fall deep into like.

*New York City

Lost and lonely
crazy late
roaming the streets of
New York City
trying to find home
immediately
searching for something
unending
something unfound in
New York City
Wishing I was
on top of the world
but I'm only in a corner
all the way
at the bottom
Rock bottom
In New York City.

*Untitled

When you talk to me
and I hear your voice
there's this thing that goes on
and I can feel you pacing
within my mind
Can't I be free
will you let me
decide if I
should objectify these feelings?
Can I be let go?
Will I stay at all?
In the abandon of your aimless gaze
and feeling lonely when you're holding me
Don't hold me back
because I'm not listening
and I've had enough...

*Untitled

Take a break
you're working too hard
and don't let yourself get in too far
you won't recognize this thing called success
till you realize it ain't the best
thing you can get.

*Untitled

I can't stop crying cause
she takes pride
in making fun of me
relishes in pointing out my flaws
and in making me see
that I am worth nothing
that I don't deserve to live
another day on my dirty ground
that I don't deserve to have
another day of making mistakes
She has made my insides
turn upside down
and my world an earthquake
But the most interesting thing to me
is that each day when I wake
in my mirror I can see
that girl's tired face
crying out in misery.

*The Beach

I want to be
back at the beach
writing in my journal
with the sun beating
down on my shoulders
Wanting to be
wading in the waves
of these seas
and in the oceans
I wish to be back in
the sun's embrace
sunburned
and not caring
about the sand in my hair
the salt in my eyes
and
oblivious to
the upcoming winter...

*Burning Pages

I saw burning words
in the wrathful revenge of last night
a precious writer's time and talent
all in a few minutes gone to waste
smoke billows and rises into the air
with words and thoughts wrapped into the mist
of flaming pages
people screaming out things
about what is written in these books
condemning the ideas
that are so artistically represented
So all I can think
as I choke on the thick smoke
is how all these letters put together
can cause such a riot
in such a quiet town.

*Untitled

Can't say I don't begin to feel restless
when you're kissing on my neck
wishing there was so much more
than living in this constant heck
Banging my head against
these inside walls I'm stuck in
I can't get rid of you
because I'm still enthralled with
the idea of you falling in love
with more than me, my whole body
but yet I wonder why that's all I
think of, if I say that we could never be
I think I might be going mad
with this weight on my chest
or maybe I'm just staying here
'cause right now, you're the best.

*Untitled

Return to me
my innocence
the days when I didn't care
how curvy my hips were
how curly my hair was
the days where I didn't know
what the fuss was all about
what was going down
yes, the days where I never worried about
how hard life would become
how hard being a teenager would ever be.

*Betrayed

There must've been something in the air that day
things wanted to go awry in every way
but you and her must've topped the cake
When I saw you at the park sucking face
My best friend and my boyfriend,
in the middle of town
Two people who had promised
they would never let me down
And now look at this pair who to my face lied
Never thought of me when they decided to be sly.

*Untitled

I'm always up
up late at night
wondering if
if this feels right
Can't recognize
the truth no more
what is right
what is pure
Things have changed.

*Please

I rest my head on your shoulder
thinking about us getting older
how life changes each and every day
how things can be given or taken away

You try and assure me that it'll be alright
that we'll still talk,
that I'm the only girl in your eyes
I want to believe you, but the future seems bleak
I kiss your lips as a tear trails down my cheek

You must have fun, try and have a good stay
Go for what you want, always stand unafraid
Remember that my heart has only one key
Don't forget what we have, and don't forget me.

*Untitled

Sticky skin
always welcomes a chill breeze
when days are scorching
and nights and are burning
and nothing can save you
but autumn.

*Macy and Tommy

Macy and Tommy play outside
in the wind
I watch as I sip sip sip my tea
brings me back to the old memories
of you and me hanging by that willow tree
Young and amusing, never thinking of the future
and what it might do to you, to me, to all of us
rid us of our energy, take the fun out of everything
make us worry about things called problems
every single day, break away from each other
and never think of anyone but ourselves
that's what life does to you, but only if you let it
I hope Macy and Tommy stay the same
I hope I hope I hope they don't change.

*Untitled

I'm sitting here in class
wanting to drill through my brain
I hope tomorrow turns out different I say
But today's tomorrow
and it feels just the same.

*Euphoria

A day without a care
You playing with my hair
Good music to my ears
Skating with you near
Us talking for 3 hours
You bringing me white flowers
Writing another poem
Calling you on the phone
A night at the *café*
A day of joyous play
Holding your hand
You being my man
Laughing all night long
Us dancing to a song
Looking at the stars
Us chilling in your car
A campfire big and bright

Being up all night
Swimming in the sea
Having you close to me
Breakfast in my bed
Tender words you said
How you make me swoon
Falling into you
Watching a good movie
Acting so unruly
Sleeping in till noon
Gazing at the moon
Warm blankets on a cold day
Telling stories around the fireplace
A dinner date for two
The way your body grooves
You and I together
a Euphoria shared forever.

*Untitled

I want to
believe you
every word you say
But contradiction
and selfish diction
is all I can find in you today
I wish we could be better
maybe even together
from where we are right now
Yet it's blistering
hoping and waiting
that someday you'll make a vow
I can't stay
holding on this way
you dragging me along
Your words are explosive
in case you haven't noticed
they make me feel so wrong
At times I would like
a sharp new knife
to pierce it through my heart
The way we were
the way it occurred
that's why we had to part.

9/16/03

*Please 2

Happy or sad, heh I'm in between
how could I go on without your shoulder to lean
you're not here and that's what kills
there are late lonely nights
where I can't stop the chills

You're so far away and I cannot resist
trying to get you back home,
so I can give you a kiss
So we can talk all night,
and I can look in your eyes
but I would feel bad knowing
what you left behind

This is harder than I thought
but I guess I must deal
there's no other person who
understands how I feel
but until you come back, I'll be standing strong
waiting for the man I love,
who I missed all along.

*Untitled

I have my days
my moments where I shine
brighter than others
My moments where I don't feel low
lost
uncomfortable and afraid
I have my moments
when I have the capability
to soar.

*Standing Out in the Crowd

I stand out
like a fluorescent light
on a dark street
tonight
I'm standing around
Hope I don't look
too desperate or
out of place
I believe
that someday this will change
One day.

10/31/03

*My Heart

I carry your heart inside my hands
trying not to squish it or hurt it
You've got my heart not in the palm
of your hand but under the sole of
your foot, crushing it every step you take.

*Not Tonight

Put the blame on
someone else this time
Please
help me
not to cry
hold me tight
and don't let go
not tonight
Spare me the drama
save it for someone
who cares
Don't let my tears fall
Please
I don't want to fight
I don't want to hurt
not tonight
I need to brace
myself
for what you're gonna say
and afterwards
I know you'll be watching
Please
Stay away
don't follow me
tonight's not the night
for this to fly
so please I beg
No, not tonight
not tonight.

*Broken Thoughts

Broken thoughts
surround me and my mind
I don't know where to start
Where should I begin
Why should I have to explain myself
or the things that I did
Broken thoughts
inside my mind
Broken thoughts
I harvest inside
When will it be time
to let go
Tonight I lie back
thinking of you
everything's broken
so instead my dreams take over
broken thoughts surrounding
and clouding, my head.

*Untitled

Wanting out
of this life
breaking down
deep inside
In the middle of the night
I awake
so simply swayed
by my heartache
And I try to find
a reason why
you wanted no compromise
you're full of lies
I walk
away
down the moonlit
pathway
and analyze
these past few days
I saw your face
and I knew you didn't care
that I was standing there
so that was the end
I stood on the ledge and
jumped as I drew my final breath
then hit the ground and bled to death.

*It's Cool

I'm an honest and loyal girl.
I don't ever trip or get crazy -
I'm cool.

We can chill and talk all day.
We make each other feel good -
We're cool.

You love me
like no other has
You are precious to me and you're great -
You're cool.

*Watching

I watch your feet
they step step slide
I watch as you
slip into the night
I watch the sand
dance through your hair
I watch you
'cause you're beautiful
and I can't help but stare.

*Untitled

You make my heart want to cry
You make my soul want to scream
I want to lie down and close my eyes
and pretend that this is all a dream

So much more out there to see
And we hold ourselves right here
You always say sweet words to me
that makes it so there's nothing to fear

Someday we'll see how this all ends
Whether this was all worth the time
I wonder if we'll just stay friends
or if I walk away with your heart,
and you with mine.

*Untitled

I look at you
from across the restaurant table
we've talked on the phone
many a time
pulled off so easily
But now it's obvious
that you're making me nervous
maybe I should call you sometime.

*Untitled

This never happened to me before
a guy that I thought I adored
had fell for me with both arms out
I realize he's a guy I could do without
This feeling faded within a day
probably as fast as the day it came
Can't really look at him anymore
without asking myself "Am I really sure?"
Now everything I do feels wrong
'cause I think anything could lead him on
I was lost and confused previously
half completely sure, half not really
He's the only guy I've crushed on that
has even liked me a little back
I think I've learned my lesson
No, there ain't no use in messin'
I'm glad that I took the time
to see that he's just not the guy
He has the looks and everything
yes, he's a great guy, just not for me.

*Untitled

Last time
we arrived
at the beach
You swam and
got sand in your eyes
We went to eat
at some rundown diner
You let me have your lemonade
It was such a treat
We walked home
and fell asleep
immediately
in our bathing suits.

*Cry

I don't think
you know
what it is to cry
So I suggest that you
don't waste your time
You are so good at
going around
and making
people hurt
and
making people
cry.

*Untitled

It was dark
you were hot
I was cold
you were not
often told
that you looked good
I'm sure they should
have let you know
a while ago
'cuz I would have
but I'm just bad
Nothing more
nothing less
but your attractiveness.

*Fresh New Day

fresh new day
sun is out
beautiful breeze
we walk
hand in hand
keeping our souls warm
feels like we are young
watch the children play
all day long
we laugh
we enjoy the sunlight
that has entered our home
the flowers are
passionately bright and
blooming
we watch the trees sway
all day
long
you pick a flower
and give it to me
we've enjoyed so much
all on this one day
fresh new day
begins again.

*Untitled

There's enough color in a strand
its softness
to keep me mesmerized with the hue
I'm relentless
I push and shove through these waves
I'm careless
to face it all before me
I'm fearless
your words bring me back to day
and suddenly
I'm faceless.

*Well

I just wanna know
when things will start going well.
Tell me in time so I can prepare myself.
I have to get past the fact
that I can never be with you.
You're far too odd for me,
but still appealing as can be.
It's a complicated story I'd rather not tell.
All I wanna know is
when things will start going well.

*Never Until Tonight

I'm scared, alright
even though you hold me tight
making sure the time is right
never until tonight
Your style, your smile
helping make the night worthwhile
will you be mine, check the time
never until tonight
You're sexy, I'm lonely
can you make my body scream
create this moment with me
never until tonight

*Untitled

Today you said I looked pretty
all said in vain I see
because in my heart I know
that she will always be
more than I could ever reach
I don't think she's as darling
as you make her out to seem
she's the best thing in everything
if that's what you believe
I don't care that she wears
your engagement ring
I know why you're with her
it's because you're not with me.

*Smitten

I lay low on the couch
watch as your mouth speaks vowels
I'm so comfortable with you
I walk past and say "hi"
watch as your eyes dart down
I'm so attracted to you
I laugh 'cuz you can do no harm
watch as your arms slip around me
I'm so glad to be your girl.

*I Wish I Wasn't Here

I wish I wasn't here

I wish I was being swept away
in the arms of some lover
Dancing loosely as the city lights hover

Talking 'bout this that or anything
Driving letting the breeze work its way in

Kicking back and relaxing in vacation sun
Under the moon
watching the waves in the ocean

Laughing with friends all around
Listening to music, so deafening the sound

Breaking away from the walls of reality
I wish I wasn't here, don't be mad at me.

*Untitled

You arrived
I acted shy
You paused and smiled
before you said hi
music was blaring
my hips were moving
your eyes followed
my dirty dancing
you stood by
the wall all night
I kept an eye on you
you kept an eye
on the time
minutes became hours
and I awaited our dance
I walked over and asked
and you said "Sorry, can't"
so I brushed it off
and waved goodbye
hoping that next time
you'd do more than just say hi.

*Untitled

Never mind the rain that's pouring
let's make love until the morning
feel my kisses traced on your skin
let out all the love I have within
Hold me close hot flesh against flesh
Scream out 'cuz I don't know what's next
I smile, but my breath is taken away
I try to take it all in, come what may
As each second subsides, I feel the burn
I reach out, it's for your body I yearn
two hearts are beating, chest against chest
Love is always better
when your lover is impressed.

*Untitled

And I write
and I am
what I'll be
when I wrote
out the song
or the book
or the poem
that took me
where it did
success is me
when I write.

*Brick

I see the wall
full of brick
I wonder what's contained
inside this building
tons of people
little people
all crowded
into small rooms
trying to live their lives
in a brick building.

*Candle

Will you light a candle for me?
Light it in my memory
the memory of me inside
your mind where all your thoughts reside
You strike the match and light the wick
I ask of you, let me unstick
the loss of us, the hurt from me
erase it, let it all release
the pain and all the games I played
let them burn within the flame
And as you watch the light wind down
you'll finally know that I am out.

*Untitled

Your misty eyes tell me that you've been crying
You try to dispel that thought but you're lying
You keep to yourself I know you're mad though
You put on a happy face I can see through those
You say you're fine but I hear your screaming
I ask can we talk, you say you're leaving
You say you're working hard to make him change
but no matter how hard you try
he'll stay the same
until he sees that what he's doing is wrong
you need to get out, move on and be strong.

*Amusement

The lights
the whirl and twirl
the heights and thrills
of amusement park rides
during summertime
cotton candy
hot dogs and soda pop
funnel cakes and candy rocks
the Ferris wheel & go-carts
makes me feel my
heart has stopped
the wind in your hair
and screams in the air
makes me feel carefree
and a little scared.

*Untitled

People look
but never really see
Passing glances say nothing and
no one knows what you mean
People shuffle, passing by
ignoring the ones that around them
You flash a quick smile at a stranger
just to see them turn away.

*Untitled

When day turns to dark
you're right by my side
forever my man
in you I can confide
you're precious like no other
I love you more every day
I hold you dear to me
in every possible way
So this one goes out to you
my man, my greatest friend
together we are unbreakable
you and I, until the end.

*Untitled

You let out a whisper
saying you feel close to me
and I hear you believe
forever isn't long enough for us
But in truth
we are light years apart
Whose are these words
that I never before knew?
Darling,
make my confusion
lay to rest.

*Untitled

When you're tucked away
in some other place
I'll be the one to pull you out
and here I'll stay
Don't be scared
I'll be there
by your side
I'll stand
I know you'll be
wherever I am
Don't get lost
in the crowd
I will be here
I'll hold it down
When you win or lose
I'll be right there
rooting you on
showing you I care.

*Untitled

There are the ones that strike me silent, asleep
The ones that make my heart skip beats
The ones who on them keep my eyes locked
The ones that make their dance moves rock
The ones who can talk for hours and hours
The ones who promise candy and flowers
The ones who say they'll buy out the store
The ones who say "I love you more."

*The Odd Ones

I find peace in you
cause there's none in me
found a love that's true
though very hard to see
took a walk outside
but I hate the cold
let the shy subside
cause you've made me bold
and when night comes
we'll try to sleep
thinking about the odd ones
like you and me.

*Number Ones

Hearing those number 1's play
brings me back to the old days
back when I had different ways
it's crazy how my life has changed
and what has still remained the same

Hearing those number 1's go on and play
reminds me of life in the game
all the hearts I threw away
messed around and had no shame
only worried about the next stage

Hearing those number 1's play
makes me remember what I used to say
walking around never fazed
thinking that no one could make
my world turn round and make me pay.

*Untitled

Lights ablaze
the spotlight is on us
we move and
take advantage of
the situation
the attention
our eyes meet
our lips kiss
and steal the show.

*We Talk

We talk slow and softly
about everything but
what must remain
unsaid. We walk along
surface streets, lined
sidewalks with enough
space in between us
too far to hold hands.
We smile inside but barely
glance toward the other
resisting the urge to
stare longingly into
those eyes. We talk slow
and softly about everything
but what must
remain unsaid...

*Untitled

A solitary guy
captures my attention
Solid
Focused
On the train
He rides along in silence
sharply dressed
and unaware
that his presence
makes me stare and
wonder what the
look in his eye
really cries
I'm taken
He seems to possess
real intelligence
His frame steps towards me
captivating
I follow with my gaze
wanna get inside his mind
I lean closer
overwhelmed with wonder
and finally
I reach to tap his shoulder
and watch as he walks past.

*Let Me

Gimme a chance
to go inside
to read and write
between the lines
to hear your voice
at every moment
to feel your touch
because I yearn for it
to experience the magic
of your mind
to hear all the stories
that you can find
to love you with
all I can give
so that I can breathe
and finally live.

*Fear

Fearful of you
and the things that you bring
the things that you show me
are all untried and
you're losing me
in a cloud of complex simplicity
You enrapture me
when you touch me
and you still hold me
even after you've released me
The things you whisper
when no one's listening
possess my thoughts
and cease my heartbeat
you push me to the edge
and I'm fearful
but you promise you'll catch me
if I ever fall for you.

*Dangerous

I lay on the cool sand
the midnight sky is
twinkling and asking
What are we doing here?
Where are we going?
There's sand in my hair
you're in my heart
love doesn't feel like it used to
and I look at you
in your eyes I search for you
don't you see we're spiraling
into self-inflicted defeat?
Waves wash over everything
I need you here with me
I hope that you feel the same
I close my eyes and slip away

*The Ex

I saw you last weekend
you're back in town again
threatening to hurt me
and destroy my life completely
But I've recovered from you
so tough now
even you couldn't cut through
I'm not gonna play your games
or get into that mess again
I don't need the waste of time
I don't need you on my mind.
Why can't you leave me alone?
I've learned 'not all that glitters is gold'
I messed up for being with you
But it's been done
can't change
my days as a fool.

*Intrigue

You see me here
I look at you
you keep staring
I wonder why
and what you're thinking
your eyes seem focused
you look attractive
I'm surprised a girl like me
has got your attention
so you've got me thinking
that you and I
could be something
I wonder...

*Our Demise was No Surprise

I couldn't break down your silent stand
I couldn't force you to take my hand
My head and heart ache and I feared
that I'd fade away not having you here
Pain doesn't even begin to define
fine just doesn't feel so fine
Your selfish dreams and all that it seemed
to come down to in the end
the problems I once knew
arose from the pit of neglect
an engagement I hurriedly left
All of this confusion is truly felt
before your eyes I wept and knelt
begging for truth and everything
for all the lies to be clarified
I was looking through to empty eyes
and a sinister smile underneath "Hi"'s
The words that were spoken and actions that hurt
all your previous intentions had lost their worth
I can almost picture it
the blur is clearing bit by bit
You ask me to join your sadistic waterfall
"cry my tears with me, this is our downpour"
but you were never there to listen when I called
and I'm not exactly sure if I can take anymore.

*Touch

Oh
the joy of your fingertips
gliding along the curves
of my body
sends me into a realm
past complete bliss
Oh
how I would do
anything
for that touch of yours that
I long for so much
Oh
I feel you
and I love you
and touch is the best sense
the one that makes
my body tense
The only sense
that makes sense
in my universe
and your absence.

*Heat

The summer heat
brings my face
to a bronzy red flush
Is it the temperature
that's got me this restless?
It's too hot of a night
to stay cooped up inside
I must leave
I must lead
my crowd downtown
The car is trailing on the wind
the smoke melts into the sky
Our minds are racing
we are escaping
and we talk like we're yelling
friends along for the ride
The heat seeps into the vehicle
through the slightly cracked windows
voices chitter chatter and echo
as a breeze blows
We walk the busy sidewalks
noisily without care
and our voices quiet
in the midst of
Italian ices
as we surrender
to the fire in the air.

*Heavy

Everything feels heavy
when you're all over me
I can't tell if that's a good thing

You say you really feel me
over the phone calls that
trail from night to morning

And I don't want to admit it
But I'm falling and it looks steep

You lay it on heavy
especially when you kiss me
I can't tell what you're wondering

As the time adds up and the days go by
I don't know what we're becoming
although I'm sure we're completely crazy

And I don't want to admit it
But I'm falling and the air feels heavy.

*Regrets

Six months ago
I said goodbye to you
cursed the ground you walked on
and said I hated you
I then embarked on
my anti-you revolution
But now I'm feeling so remorseful about
the way I acted, how I stomped you out
And it hurts me even more
that you look so happy
without me
I peek through
your tall glass windows
every night on the sly
when you can't tell
that I'm checking up on you
it's a nightly thing
I can't help it
because in actuality
I'm still in love with you
and I know you probably think
this can't be true
but I'm honestly
caught up in missing you.

*Superstore

He's perverse and too open
but I'm still attracted
He smells incredibly
good
though he talks filthy
Smooth hair and sweet lips
though his 5 o'clock shadow
is tipping six
But this truth is
I want him
all of him
Clean skin
All of his 20 year old
magnificence
in my possession
He's unaffected by
gaping mouths and wide eyes
staring in awe and surprise
because he's beautiful and
just a little out of line
I know if he was mine
he'd treat me like a queen
but I'd have to put up with certain things

"Take it or leave it" he says
and I know that he says what he means
He's the center all the time
but to me he's just fine
He reads all philosophy
can talk the ears off of me
He's thoroughly intelligent
sexy and scarred and intense
He never settles down
he's always wired out
Thing is, I still want him
I can repair him
I can repair him
But he's fireworks
and I'm a candle
I don't know if it can work
if he's more than I can handle
but I only know his name and age
not much more
he's the guy that I eye
every time
I go
to the superstore.

*Higher Heights

Life is sweet
when I'm imagining
our tangled bodies
kissing hugging loving
in the kitchen or
in between our sheets
How do I feel
when I feel
like I'm falling
deeper and you're seeping
into my pores and my being
and my life and every second
of every day that I might
contemplate
taking this to higher heights
where you and I
can unify
and I can show you
everything
a midst feeling so high
You're my heart and my soul
but will you ever know?
So it's time
to express the stir in my heart

and my mind
Whenever you're close
my surroundings shine
into something divine
Can I feel you?
hard knocks heart stops
all that you've got
to throw at me
You're all in me
when I sleep
and when I sigh
and when I blink
I can't get my mind right
to think about proper things
concerning you and me
drowning in ecstasy
moaning and groaning
uncontrollably
And I have gratitude
because you know exactly
what you're doing
but that's just in my dreams
give me some reality.

*Untitled

You reflect me
praise me for what I possess
never mention what I lack
Show me
I am my only everything
See in me
all that I can become
View me
for all that I am
faults and imperfections
jagged edges and soft corners
beauty real and imagined
open space and closed doors
Gloriously complex
yet simple and refined
You raise me up
from the lows
And rescue me from
the throes of emotion
You lead me
to wise conclusions
and comfort
When I cried
you held me
And every day
you hold me.

*Impossible

Kiss the flame
Touch the sky
Hold in your hands
the ocean tide
Hold me gently and say
you'll stay

*A Summertime Memento

I am here wading in the still water
and I'm remembering...

Sprawled out on the grass
watching the flickering stars
So I let this summer be
and experienced a whole new world
and how we laughed and laughed and laughed
in this atmosphere that made us feel so free
We thought we were invincible
dancing in the streets
with fireflies in our souls
and fire at our feet
The way we screamed
and laughed and spoke
something I'd never seen
The night the sound of summer filled the air

the way we all sat and listened so intently
like the world stopped turning
I'd felt so placid, a self-serene
continuously on the hunt for this feeling
and there it was in front of me
so exceptional, so unique
I look at you all, and wish this could be
so forever
Hoping I could stay inside this summer
instead, time moves quick, and memories
are all you're left with
I'm surprised at the tear in my eye
disguised by my smile and a soft giggle

...And so I dive deeper into this luminescent pool
and silently say goodbye to this summer, so cool.

*Unaware of the Rain

It rained today? I asked myself
while taking a sip of my tea
If it had, I would've never known
I sat, propped up so pretty
on my window seat
surrounded, almost encased
in my oblivion
gazing outside the window
watching the wind
and listening to the soft pitter patter
of my heart
Sitting
trying to decipher what's going on in my mind
trying to sort through my ideas
I was so worked up
I hadn't known if it had rained at all.

*The Girls

There are the girls
In their dark dark tight and dirty
denim jeans
and their wavy golden locks
and sweet Southern accents
and strong personalities
So beautiful, it's disgusting
So sweet, it's sickening
with their pretty baby eyes
and innocent, sparkling smiles
and curves that could sway the wind
With their bright and showy tops
and breasts the size of mountains
perfect intellectuals
perfect manners too
There are the perfect girls
And here I sit
acting like my envy
hasn't swallowed me whole.

*Beautiful

Acceptance is what you get
when they don't understand you
and you're beautiful instead
Admittance is what you get
when they don't hear what you say
but they listen anyway
because you're beautiful
And no one cares to know
what you hold inside
much more pleasant to look
'cause you're so easy on the eyes
But this is only because you're beautiful.

*Silk Denim Suede

You're the essence of honey
and you couldn't be
ever more lovely
You are silk in fine threads
and I'm taken in
as I take you apart
You've got that tough exterior
no one could tear your heart
and even if you let them
your heart's made out of denim
a smoother surface you couldn't pull off
You're rough, but so soft
explain your motives
you must need not
'cause your body's like suede
and it makes me so hot.

*The First Time

Reminds me how easily I fell in love the first time
The first time I laid eyes on your charming guise
We walked talkative through the blindingly
    bright city streets
Hands avoiding each other since the handshake
    at first greet
My eyes followed the lapels on your sleek
    leather jacket
My hands traced the brim of your hat and then
    fell into my pockets
I remember you clutching your headphones at
    the back of Virgin
Your quiet jamming and crooning, my slowly
    advancing attraction
I think I united the divide by lacing my fingers
    in between yours
Stood near me coolly, pretending you didn't
    want something more
I wouldn't look in your eyes, afraid you'd see all
    I was too shy to say
But over some time, I saw that the words had
    reached you anyway
I adored watching you dance, your moves were
    precise and perfect
I loved watching you be completely serious and
    act completely foolish
It was getting tangled and I couldn't help but
    have felt what I was feeling

Through touches, passionate first kisses, and all
that I was seeing
And although we were cautious, I knew I had
positively fell from high
The night our souls touched and I felt every
fiber in my body sigh
We paid no attention to what loomed outside
your Brooklyn apartment
We were too busy, too involved in everything
our love meant
Touching every muscle, between every curve,
my stomach in knots
All this time and I never knew ecstasy was this hot
Our love was in motion one year and four
months, trust me I remember it clear
We were coming to a close and although I
hadn't felt it before, I knew it was fear
You said we were too young, lines were blurred,
what it was, what it wasn't
We parted ways, lived our separate lives, and in
time I kinda forgot about it
Just last week I saw you, the one who filled my
little heart with sorrow
I was so surprised and yet so delighted, I
couldn't even utter the word "Hello"
Throughout conversation and your smile, I
noticed you still have those same eyes
The stare and the grin and the words that
remind me why I fell in love the first time.

*Concept of a Broken Marriage

She understands on those nights
that the snow falls soft
When he cannot give her reassurance
that he's still in love
The nights that he cannot bear to look at her
and instead scoffs
And it is pain that always plagues
the heart he once stole
It is hard when she is losing grip
of the hand she longs to hold
She offers him her shoulder
and gets nothing but his cold one
His hands barely ever touch her
and it feels like she's coming undone
It is evident she feels the lack of everything
that a true relationship is supposed to bring
He storms inside the house
and gives her a look of earnest hate
There is nothing she can offer him
that will change his tragic state
And she promises this hurts worse
than the punches and the put-downs
that her Father used to give her
when she was young and acted out
She cries on the evenings he pushes dinner away
and rushes out of the room with nothing to say
She doesn't want him to tell her
he's just not hungry, hell

it would be nice if for once he explained
how he really felt
The truth may hurt but not more
than the assumptions she makes
She doesn't even want him to put on a smile
and pretend it's not fake
In truth, she wishes she could
silence his temper, temper his silence
Make his evil actions disappear,
help clear out all the nonsense
She knows that inside of her lies
the girl he once loved without
the perfection and expectations
he constantly holds above her now
She wonders and damn does she hope
and false hopes they will always be
thinking about what happened to the calm,
collected man she knew at 18
Lying in bed cold and alone asking herself
what else could possibly go wrong
Looking at him and her reflection in the mirror
knowing she doesn't belong
She is done pining for him, wanting him,
and making excuses for him
One sunny morning she grabbed her things
and left a note all done on a whim
She turned the radio up as she rode down
the highway and into the night

Started to cry when she realized he had
never been about her, or her life
It had only been altercations, disappointments,
a complete wreck
Sadness in her eyes and an empty wish
for change he hadn't come to yet
She decided she would make up for all the time
her husband cost and stole
All vows lost as her wedding ring was tossed
into the speeding stretch of blurry road.

*Unreal

Last week the war begun
I can't believe that you have won
I don't think the soldier in me exists
your expressions of aggression still persist
The wounds in me have been revealed
I'm taken by pain that feels unreal

When you look at the one
you thought you loved
And you see everything but
something you were once a part of
Tell me how it feels
say it feels unreal
so surreal

The other day reality set in
After the end how does one begin
sometimes I feel as if I can't go on
silent words are telling me be strong
I hope and pray my soul will heal
I'm walking away and it feels unreal

When you look at the one
Who you gave the world to
And you see everything but
someone who deserved you
Tell me how it feels
say it feels unreal
So surreal

*Surfacing

Get off
take whatever you need to take from me
And leave
I need some time to think
I'm recognizing you were never there with me

Cuz I'm finally surfacing, darling
And let me say
I've never felt this way
I feel my best

Make off
Steal whatever you need to steal from me
And leave soon
I need some time to live
I'm realizing you were never there for me

Cuz I'm finally surfacing, darling
And let me say
I've never felt this way
I feel my best

Weren't you supposed to
make me feel better
Instead you tore my life apart
forever
or that's what I thought...

Cuz I'm finally surfacing, darling
And let me say
I've never felt this way
I feel my best

Said I'm finally surfacing, darling...

*Untitled

You said to meet you
tomorrow
at a little past noon
So I walked the three blocks
and entered the room
The lighting made you look so fine
then you walked over and said "Well, hi."
And I must've fell right into your embrace
'cause it all felt right
nothing out of place
We look good together
it's obvious
I know
Side by side I'm sure we could
steal the whole dang show
I looked in your eyes
and you pulled me in for a kiss
my mind was racing
as we touched our lips
And as you grabbed my hand
and we walked out
I felt my smile stretch wide
and my heart shout.

*Untitled

You wake up more tired than ever
to the stale air in your tiny room
and head downstairs
to eat some "breakfast" at 3PM.
And all that's left behind
is some old rice from last night
that nearly breaks your teeth
Your stomach feels like it's rotting
cause the butterflies are flying
because of that one night
that wasn't even a big deal
but is still on your mind...

*Summer

Summer, summer
Always summer
There lies summer in your eyes
summer in your heart
and summer in your hair
Summer is the heat of life
and summer adds plenty of spice.

*Basic

Keep it simple
Nice and easy
No complications
Nothing extraordinary
All laid-back
None of the extravaganzas,
just basic.

*Tears

the tears that stream
that moisten the skin
are those the same tears
that I'm crying for him?

*Untitled

Let's dance and drink the night away
'cause we can't talk no more
And I can't wait to ask
I can't wait to see
Are your feelings that strong?
Are you falling for me?
Right now I don't know
So let's just dance.

*Peace

It's this simple thing
an intangible essence
only seen in the still
waters of the sea and
soft light that gleams
in the dawn
in the dusk and
through twilight serene
It's in the eyes of the hopeful
and souls of the young
and carefree

It's a desire of
the righteous
the lovely
the suppressed
and the ugly
It's in budding rosebuds
and sunny powdered skies
It's in the breeze
In acts of sanction
and in sighs of relief
of those in need

None in restless sleep
rare in the everyday
Absent in the worries we keep and
insignificant to those in power today
None in the red white and blue
sweet land of liberty
that's NOTHING
when across the Atlantic Sea
there's bombings and infantries
slaughtering the unsuspecting
and full of sunken armies.

It's felt in calm embraces
and for saddened faces
It shines throughout years of
everlasting love
It's in silence and in truth and
amidst soaring doves

It is somewhere lost in time
irrefutably divine
It's in the heavens and hearts of the deceased
And when that time arrives
may one forever rest in peace.

About the Author

The author began writing at the age of 11, after finding her older brother's mesmerizing journal and saying to herself "I can do that too!" Elle started blogging on xanga.com as a teenager, created the lifestyle blog 'Known as Blue' in 2009 and published her first work—the poetry collection "Sixteen"—in the spring of 2019. She has appeared on the popular beauty site 'Into The Gloss' and has had a tweet printed in Oprah Winfrey's 'O Magazine'. Elle enjoys coffee, dark dramas and R&B music, has three more projects in the works and a love-hate relationship with New York City, where she resides.

Keep up with Elle Blue at:
www.KnownasBlue.com

Support her work at:
www.Patreon.com/KnownasBlue